THE SHY GUY'S GUIDE
TO TALKING TO WOMEN

And Having Girls Absolutely Love You For It

.

THE SHY GUY'S GUIDE TO TALKING TO WOMEN

And Having Girls Absolutely Love You For It

By
Dominic Mann

TABLE OF CONTENTS

INTRODUCTION

I freakin' hate girls.

Okay, maybe that's not the best way to start a dating book.

But it's true. Girls are confusing and scary and make my life much, much harder.

[Insert a dramatic sigh here.]

But on the other hand, I also love girls.

A lot.

[Insert a romantic sigh here.]

In the last year I've been on 60 dates with 60 different girls. Even if you're not a professional mathematician, you can probably agree with me that that's a lot of dates. I'm definitely not the most prolific dater of all time, but I'm definitely not your average wallflower either.

At least, not anymore.

I used to be terribly shy. If you put me in the same room with a girl I'd clam up and have absolutely no idea what to do. I wouldn't open my mouth if you paid me a million dollars.

And I might very well crap my pants on the spot. Which doesn't necessarily make a great first impression.

I wrote this book for people like me. People that are great once you get to know them... but have a really hard time with first impressions and talking to new girls for the first time.

If you've got a great personality but have a hard time opening your mouth and breaking out of your shell... you're in the right place. This book will show you how to totally nail the first interaction with a girl.

Because let me tell you: the first interaction is BY FAR the most important. It's impossible to overestimate the effect a powerful first impression can have. First impressions lay the foundation for every other interaction you're going to have with that person.

I've seen this in my own life over and over again.

A couple of months ago I somehow got wrangled into doing 15 minutes of live stand-up comedy for the first time in front of 350 people. And it actually turned out really well, even though it was super last minute and I was only able to rehearse twice before going out on stage.

Afterwards I was mingling with the audience, and I ended up asking out one of the girls that I met that night. And guess what? When we went on our date, I was funnier than I've probably ever been on another date before.

She expected me to be funny, and so I was.

And now every time I see her, I'm somehow naturally funnier than I normally am.

I'm telling you, first impressions are powerful.

I've also seen the same thing happen in reverse. One time I met this guy while I was exhausted and had a really bad headache, and so I came off as really shy and reserved. And every time I see him, for some reason I become really shy, even though I'm almost never shy anymore.

It's weird.

So yeah, first impressions can be a pain in the butt. But they can also be a powerful tool. Because if you can totally nail your first interaction with a girl... well, I can almost guarantee that the second interaction will be just as amazing. And so will the third. And the fourth. And so on.

The first interaction lays the foundation for everything else that follows it.

And in fact, lots of times it will determine if there even IS a second interaction. Because if you're really bad with first impressions, chances are you won't have the opportunity to make a second impression.

But don't worry.

This book will ensure that you never have to worry about making a bad first impression. I'm going to show you how to totally nail the entire first interaction, and leave girls dying for you to ask them out.

It all comes down to three simple steps:

First: I'll teach you how to get "in the zone" and skyrocket your self-confidence.

Second: I'll teach you how to open up and be your true self in public.

Third: I'll teach you how to converse like a pro and never run out of things to talk about.

And that's it. If I can successfully teach you how to do those three things, you'll be able to go to a bar or a party or whatever TONIGHT, and have the time of your life.

I'm telling you, it can be done.

A little over a year ago I implemented the 3 techniques I'm about to show you, and it totally changed everything for me. My social life is 100% better than it was this time last year.

It wasn't necessarily always super easy, but it is definitely possible. If I can do it, so can you.

So let's do it.

Rock n' roll, baby.

CHAPTER 1:
MINDSET

Ugh.

Mindset.

Am I right?

Chances are that the last thing you want to hear about right now is freaking "mindset". And luckily for you, I'm on your side. I wanna barf whenever I hear the word mindset.

I know that a lot of other dating books are really big on mindset. They talk about how success with a girl is 80% in your head, and 20% everything else.

I disagree with that.

I'd completely flip-flop it, actually. I'd say that success is probably only 20% mindset, and 80% everything else.

But it's important to get the 20% out of the way before you move onto everything else. It's kind of hard to win a race if you only run 80% of the way.

Unless you cheat. I suppose you could take a shortcut that allows you to skip 20% of the race and win by a long shot.

But I'm not exactly sure how to tie that into a dating analogy.

Ha. *Analogy.* I have to be careful how I use that word in a dating book. I'm used to writing self-help books, so you'll have to forgive me. I just realized how much fun I can have with that word in the dating market.

Ahem.

Anyways. Let's move on before things get, uh, messy. Or at least before they get messier than they already are. Sorry.

PRETEND EVERYONE IS TERRIFIED OF YOU

I used to have terribly low self-esteem.

I would obsess over my weaknesses and shortcomings, and that absolutely destroyed my sense of self-worth. I didn't know how to separate myself from my problems. I thought of myself as a problem.

And as you can probably guess, this made it pretty hard to meet new people and talk about myself and try to impress them.

But then one day, I accidentally discovered this fun little hack.

I don't remember exactly when I came up with the idea. But I did. And it revolutionized the way I acted around new people.

Every time I met someone new, I'd pretend that they were super intimidated of me. And that made life approximately 1,000 times easier. I don't know why this works so well, but dang. It really does.

And it's super easy to implement. If you just take one second to remember this one technique every time you go up to talk to someone new… that's all it takes. Just one second to adjust your mindset. And it will work wonders in your dating life. I can guarantee you.

And it works outside of first interactions as well. Whenever I'm intimidated to talk to someone, regardless of whether or not it's the first time I've met them, I'll just do some quick mental gymnastics and convince myself that they're actually intimidated of me.

And so far, it's worked every single time. This technique never fails to shoot my self-confidence through the roof. Which makes talk to a hot chick for the first time much easier.

If you want to make a good first impression, your number one priority should be to get your self-confidence up. Because you won't be able to implement any of the other techniques in this book if you're feeling super crappy about yourself.

But this one technique is all you need to skyrocket your self-esteem.

Now let's talk about how to get over shyness…

KEEP THINGS IN PERSPECTIVE

You're a liar.

A big, fat, filthy liar.

It's not your fault though. Because we all do it. Every single person reading this book is a compulsive liar. It's human nature to lie to ourselves. And so we do. All the frickin' time.

Even if you've never told a single lie in your entire life, I can guarantee you that you lie to yourself every single day. That's just the way our brains our wired. We exaggerate every single little thing.

Think about the last time you really liked a girl. Let's imagine you told this girl one of your best jokes. And she didn't laugh. At all. The joke fell totally flat.

That's okay, right? It's not a huge deal. Jokes fall flat from time to time. Maybe the delivery was a little off, or maybe it was the wrong environment or mood setting. Whatever, right? There's a lot of things that could've gone wrong.

But that's not what you're going to think. You're going to lie to yourself. You're going to tell yourself that you're not funny. You're going to tell yourself that this girl probably hates your guts. You're going to question why she even went out with you in the first place. Maybe she was just being nice. She's probably not having any fun. You should probably just call it a night and drop her off and go home early.

I've been in this exact scenario several times before. Something small will go wrong, but I'll exaggerate it and lie to myself and think that the world is ending.

Before you walk up to a girl for the first time, it's important to understand that the world isn't going to end. Keep things in perspective. Don't lie to yourself. Understand that (especially if you're shy) you're probably going to exaggerate the small things and turn them into big things.

Don't.

This is one of the most important mindset tweaks you can ever make. When you keep things in perspective and don't lie to yourself, it's so much easier to be bold and venture outside your comfort zone. In fact, the instant you start using this technique your comfort zone will expand quite a bit.

At the risk of stating the obvious… yeah, this technique is pretty dope.

HAVE A PURPOSE

Most people are idiots.

But I suppose you already knew that. Unless, of course, you are one of the aforementioned idiots. In which case... condolences.

No, but seriously, most people are particularly... lost... when it comes to social interactions. Especially first impressions.

Most people will just walk into a first interaction without any sort of a plan or a goal or anything. Don't be like that. Know what you're there for and what you want. Be consciously aware of the purpose of each interaction. Be like a missile speeding toward a precise target.

Now, I'm not saying you should be a social robot and be super lame and boring. If a chick can tell that you've been reading a dating book, then you've failed. (We'll talk more about this later.) It's okay to be fun and spontaneous. But it's possible to be spontaneous AND goal oriented.

When you're purpose driven, you're going to succeed much faster than you will any other way. It's hard to win a race when you're not even sure which finish line you're trying to cross. (Ha. Another race(y) anal-ogy. Sorry. I'm a horrible person. You're welcome.)

But in all seriousness, if you begin with the end in mind, you're going to be much better off. Still be a real person. Don't be robotic and mechanical. But do your best to have a goal with each social interaction that you participate in.

Continuing the missile analogy, you could put a big red nose on the front of it. And some party balloons trailing out the back. And have it swerving left and right to the beat of "Saturday Night Fever" by the Bee Gees. But I digress.

This mindset tweak has helped me speed things up and allowed me to (uh, how do I say this?) put the rubber to the road much faster than I would be able to any other way.

FOCUS OUTWARDS

The vast majority of people are very self-centered. Pretty much everyone is at the center of their own universe.

Which isn't a horrible thing. I mean, it makes sense. Caring about yourself is a pretty important step to staying alive.

But if you take that same "center of the universe" attitude into the first interaction with a girl you're interested in… you're not going to make it very far.

If you really want to make a splash and get on the radar of a girl, you need to put her at the center of your universe. The most impressive thing you can do is to be impressed by her.

So many people try to hook up with girls by talking about themselves and how impressive they are. Don't be that guy. There are enough of them out there. Focus outwards instead of inwards. Temporarily remove yourself from the center of your universe. Step outside of yourself and channel all of your attention towards whoever you're talking to.

I feel like I say this every time, but this is probably the most important technique you could ever implement. This one mindset shift will make all of the difference in the world for you.

When you start focusing outwards, everything changes.

Stop worrying about that zit on your chin, and whether or not you're being funny enough, and how you're going to start paying for a gym membership. All of that stuff pales in comparison when you become selfless and focus entirely on the other person.

Try to talk about yourself as little as possible. I recommend a 60/40 ratio at the bare minimum. Preferably 70/30. I wouldn't recommend going too far below 80/20 though. It's important to give your personality a chance to shine. Just don't make it the main attraction.

It seems weird, but the more you take the focus off of yourself, the better of first impression you'll make.

Trust me on this one. Everyone loves to hang around people that treat them like they're unbelievably important. And you can be the person to make that dream come true for some lucky girl later tonight.

CHAPTER 2:
HOW TO BE YOU

Okay, here's the dealio.

You're not you.

I know that sounds weird. But trust me on this.

There's a real you, and a fake you. And chances are that you have a hard time being your real you. Especially in social settings. And *especially* in social settings that involve talking to nice young ladies for the first time.

It's just the way things are. I know what it's like. If you put me next to a fine looking young lass, one of two things would usually happen: I'd either clam up and say absolutely nothing. Or I'd say the absolute dumbest thing possible in that particular situation.

I'm not sure which was worse. Probably the latter. I can still remember the "looks" that I've received over the years. Looks of pity. Looks of surprise. Looks of disgust.

If you pulled me aside a couple of years ago and told me that someday I'd be writing a dating book... I would've laughed in your face. I didn't know how to act around girls AT ALL. I had a great personality, but I didn't know how to get that across over the course of the first interaction.

The people that liked me were the people that knew me really well. And the people that knew me really well were the people that were forced to spend a lot of time around me. Usually family.

The point is that I didn't know how to act like my *real* self whenever I'd meet a girl for the first time. Which means I made a lot of horrible first impressions, which means I didn't have many lady friends, which means I didn't go on many dates.

But all of that changed when I learned how to…

[insert dramatic music right here]

…unleash my true self.

Watch and learn.

UNDERSTAND WHO YOU ARE

I hate Prince Charming. I really do. I hate his guts.

I feel like there are so many guys out there that think they have to be absolutely perfect in every single possible way before a nice girl will be attracted to them. Which is absolute bullcrap.

You don't have to be perfect in order to find love. You don't even have to be close. Hopefully you know this. There is a girl out there that will like you just the way you are. You don't need to be Prince Charming. You don't need to have chiseled abs and a spot-on sense of humor and a buttload of money.

You just need to be you. And you need to understand that there is someone out there that will absolutely love you, just for you.

But before that can happen, you need to understand who you are. And chances are that you're not Prince Charming. You probably have a couple of weaknesses. If you're like me, then you have more weaknesses than you could ever possibly count. (One of them being math.)

And in order for you to be comfortable in revealing your true self, you need to understand what those weaknesses are. And you need to embrace them.

So many guys try to completely ignore their weaknesses. They'll shove them down as deep as they possibly can, and pretend that they don't exist. And when they meet a nice chick, they try to come off as Prince Charming. They'll pretend that they're perfect in every way. Which, as you can probably tell based on context, works every single friggin' time.

Not.

Seriously, don't pretend to be perfect. It's not worth it. No one is perfect.

Be aware of your weaknesses. Accept the fact that you have them, and be okay with that.

Now, with that said…

Don't dwell on your weaknesses. There are an equal number of guys that do this. They only see the negative in themselves. They're convinced that no girl will ever want them because of the couple of things that are wrong with them.

Don't let that happen to you.

I used to be that way, and I definitely don't recommend it.

I used to be super embarrassed because of how skinny I am. (Seriously, 6'2" and 150 pounds ain't necessarily the prettiest sight ever.) I told myself that no girl would ever be interested in me because I'm not as built as some of the other guys out there.

I didn't realize that there were girls out there that would see past that, and like me for the person I was, not just the way I looked. I couldn't see past my shortcomings.

And so when a girl would show interest in me, I'd ignore her. I'd tell myself that I was just imagining things, and that no girl would actually be interested in someone like me, because I'm not Prince Charming.

I didn't realize that I don't need to be Prince Charming. I just need to be me. And I need to find someone that likes me for me. Weaknesses and all.

Okay. Are we on the same page?

Don't dwell on your weaknesses. That won't get you anywhere. It's important to be aware of them, so that you can try to improve, but don't dwell on them. Accept the fact that there's someone out there that will like you for you. (As mushy as that sounds, it's true.)

So what should you do with this information?

I'd recommend taking a couple of minutes to sit down with a notepad and pencil. Jot down your top 3 weaknesses. Or top 5. Whatever you want to do. Take a minute to accept that these are the things you struggle with.

And then burn the paper. Or rip it to shreds or something. Don't worry about it ever again. Dwelling on your weaknesses won't do you any good.

Cool?

Cool.

Now we can move onto the second part of this whole thing.

Which is to be aware of your strengths.

It's just as important to be aware of your strengths as it is to be aware of your weaknesses.

If there's one fact that I absolutely believe with all of my heart, it's that everyone is awesome. Everyone has at least one amazing talent. I talk a lot about how people are idiots (and they are) but they're also incredible.

There are so many people out there that I really respect and admire. And not just world famous, celebrity-type people either. Even the most ordinary, totally normal people have amazing stories to tell and talents to offer.

That includes you.

I honestly believe that you are incredibly amazing. Whoever you are. It doesn't matter. You have some awe-inspiring talents and strengths. And there's a person out there for you that will be totally blown away by what you can do.

Chances are there are actually a lot of people out there that'd be totally amazed by you, regardless of whether or not you consider yourself to be amazing.

But I shouldn't get carried away. I certainly don't want to get too big of a head. There are a lot of people out there in the world. The statistical probability of every single person in the world hating your guts is pretty slim. That's all I'm saying.

Even if it seems like everyone hates you, statistically speaking, there's gotta be at least one chick out there that would totally dig you.

But chances are that she lives in Mongolia or something. Sorry. It sucks to suck, I guess. (Dang, I'd make an amazing motivational speaker, wouldn't I?)

No, but seriously. Don't underestimate your strengths. You're a person. And people are great.

Now go ahead and do the same exercise that I had you do earlier. Write down your top 3-5 strengths. Accept the fact that these things are totally awesome, and there are plenty of girls out there that would be blown away by you.

Not the fake you. But the real you.

The you that has some pretty terrifying weaknesses as well as some awe-inspiring strengths.

Which brings me to my next point...

BE A REAL PERSON

Don't lie.

Don't pretend.

Don't be fake.

Just be you. I know that's probably some of the most cliché dating advice out there. But there's a reason it's cliché. Because it's important. Don't ignore it.

Don't be afraid to be a real person. A person that has weaknesses and strengths.

So many people are tempted to prop up their strengths and try to come off as impressive as possible, while simultaneously burying their weaknesses as deep as possible. Don't do that.

Being real is much more impressive than lying about being impressive.

It's going to be hard to do, but you can do it.

The point is that being your true self is gonna be tough, but you can do it. Maybe you won't get it perfect on the first try. But luckily life is full of second chances. You don't have to be perfect all at once.

Just go out tonight and do your best. And then do your best tomorrow. And the day after that. And eventually you'll get it right.

CHAPTER 3:
CONVERSE LIKE A PRO

Okay. Let's recap.

In Chapter One we talked about how to hack your mindset, so that you make sure you're as mentally and emotionally prepared as possible before you step out onto the battlefield.

In Chapter Two we talked about how to be you. The real you. Strengths and weaknesses and everything.

I'm super excited for Chapter Three. Chapter Three is where the rubber hits the road. It's where everything comes together, and you're actually able to implement all of the cool stuff we've been talking about.

Now we're gonna talk about how to talk about stuff.

If you're interested in stepping up your game and hooking chicks left and right… knowing how to carry out a halfway decent conversation is pretty important. In this chapter that's exactly what I'll show you how to do.

I promise it's not as hard as you think it will be.

Even if you've never successfully talked to a girl in your entire life, before you know it you'll be talking to EVERY girl at the bar. You won't be able to help yourself.

Because talking is actually surprisingly fun.

I wouldn't have believed you if you'd told me that a couple of years ago. Back then, talking with the opposite sex was pure agony. I'd take a torture chamber over a 10 minute conversation any day of the week.

But all that changed when I learned these 5 simple techniques to spice up your first conversation with a new girl…

IT'S ALL ABOUT THEM

I mentioned this briefly before.

But it's so absolutely critical to understand. The more you focus on the girl that you're with, the more she'll like you.

It's as simple as that.

And conversation-time is when you need to really put this into action and focus on her as much as possible.

So many guys clam up because they're not sure what to talk about, when all they need to is talk about her! Figure out what she's passionate about. Not just the things that she likes, but the things that she really, truly, deeply cares about. And then talk to her about that. For as long as possible.

I've never been much of a girlfriend guy, but I recently decided to settle-down a bit and stop going on so many dates with so many different girls. Mostly because I met this one chick that was super, super awesome and everyone else paled in comparison.

At first I had a little bit of a hard time finding things to talk about with her. But then I discovered that she's super interested in law enforcement, and is looking to become a cop. So I made it a point to talk to her about cop stuff as much as possible.

And it was amazing. She can talk about that stuff all day long, and all I have to do is sit there and listen and ask the occasional question. Easiest conversation of my life.

I'm telling you, conversations are super easy once you learn how to quickly identify the things a person is passionate about.

Every person on this planet has something that they're passionate about. And if you want to connect with them on a meaningful level, all you have to do is figure out what that thing is.

Dating is tough, but it's not rocket science.

Just remember: focus on her as much as possible.

If I ever, EVER find myself talking for more than 50% of the time, then I'm a total failure. I try to get way lower than that, if I can. If I can get the girl that I'm with to talk for 70% or 80% of the time, I'll consider it a grand success.

Obviously it's important to contribute your own opinions and allow your personality a chance to shine. But as a general rule of thumb, the more you focus on whoever you're with, the more impressed they'll be with you.

ASK THE RIGHT QUESTIONS

Questions are the meat and potatoes of any solid conversation.

If you can ask the right questions, you can have an amazing conversation with anybody. At any time. In any place.

So many people are so lame with their conversations. I swear, 90% of conversations start with "how are you tonight?" or "what's your name?".

DON'T DO THAT!!!

Be unique. If you want to set yourself apart from the competition, you need to say things they've never heard before. You need to be bold and creative.

And it's really not as hard as you think.

You can take the common conversation-starter questions that we hear all the time and twist them around.

Instead of "how are you doing?" ask "so, on a scale of 1-10, how are you doing today? And why?".

I can't tell you how many times I've met totally awesome girls by starting a conversation this way. It's super easy to do, it's probably something they haven't heard before, and it almost always leads to an interesting conversation.

But that's just the tip of the iceberg.

If you're walking up to a girl you've never met before, instead of saying "hi, what's your name?", try sitting down and saying "okay, I've never met you, but I'm going to try to guess your name. You cool with that?"

Then just start guessing away. After 3 or 4 guesses, ask her for the first letter. If you guess it right away, then it comes off as a pretty cool trick. And if you totally fail and aren't even close, she'll usually laugh and think it's hilarious. Either way it's a win for you.

This is a super fun game that works almost every time. And it's so easy to do. It's just takes a little bit of creativity.

I'm telling you, NEVER start a conversation the "normal" way again. Be creative. Ask weird questions. It'll get you places you never dreamed of before.

Here are some of my personal favorites:

- What's your favorite thing about life?
- If you had to rate your life on a scale of 1-10, overall, what would it be?
- If you were on the run from the law, where would you go?
- What color is your toothbrush? What does that say about your personality?
- What's one thing you've always wanted to try, but never have?
- What's the most embarrassing thing that has ever happened to you?

That last one is really great at breaking the ice and getting through to people that are a little too formal and reserved. It almost always leads to hilarious stories that are a lot of fun and inspire plenty of laughter.

If you know how to ask good questions, starting a conversation isn't as hard as you think it is. And if you can get a conversation started, you can easily keep it going for as long as you need just by focusing on her as much as possible.

And coming up with creative questions isn't as hard as you think it is. I'd recommend you stop reading this book and take a couple of minutes to come up with 10 creative conversation-starters of your own. Right now. It's kinda fun to come up with them, actually.

Or even if you just want to steal mine or Google "questions to start interesting conversations" or whatever, here's the important thing to remember: you absolutely need to ditch small talk. Forever.

Small talk is super lame, and anybody can do that.

You need to start conversations in a way that only you can.

HAVE FUN

Once you've got a conversation started, it's important to keep it going.

The best way to do this?

Don't stress out. So many people are too serious when they have conversations with girls they like. Don't be like that.

Have fun. Loosen up a bit. Be bold. Say things you normally would be too scared to say.

If you ever have a conversation with a girl and you don't push yourself outside of your comfort zone at least a little bit, you're doing something wrong.

That's always been my philosophy, and so far it's worked out pretty well. Sure, every once in awhile it'll backfire. But in my experience girls tend to appreciate it when you're willing to be bold and say things that scare the crap outta you.

Obviously there needs to be a balance. There are some lines that you shouldn't cross. But it's okay to have a little bit of fun. You don't need to talk about super serious stuff all the time.

If you're having trouble with this, you can fall back on the "pretend that she's super intimidated of you" mindset technique from Chapter One. That sucker will shoot your self-confidence right back up to where it should be.

RECOGNIZE THE PEAK

This is one of the very hardest techniques to implement. But it's absolutely essential.

Let's say that you've had a totally amazing conversation with a totally amazing girl. Let's say that you talked about tons of fun stuff that both of you were super passionate about. Let's say that you really *clicked* and you want to get married and have kids and a white picket fence together.

If this ever happens to you, there is one simple thing that you need to do: call it quits.

You should always end a conversation when it's at the peak. The perfect time to end a conversation is when it's going great and you don't want it to end.

Like I said, this is a freaking *hard* technique to implement. Because when you're in the middle of a great conversation, obviously the only thing you want is to keep it going.

But I can promise you that there is a peak to every conversation. There is a point where it has reached the highest heights that it ever will. Sure, there might still be a lot of other great things that you can talk about. But none of them will be able to match the peak.

And if you end a conversation when you're at the peak, that will be what is freshest in her mind when you leave. And that will make her want to pursue a second conversation. And maybe a third. And a fourth. And maybe eventually you guys will take up some extracurricular activities that don't involve talking.

Such as jogging.

Obviously.

No, but seriously. If you don't want a conversation to end, that's the perfect time to cut it off. And if you *are* ready for a conversation to end, then you've let it linger on for too long.

Don't be afraid to be ruthless, efficient, and deadly.

Being nice never got nobody nowhere.

Actually, that's a lie. Because karma is totally a real thing. But yeah. You know what I mean.

Don't be afraid to cut conversations off ruthlessly.

This is a hard technique to follow, but it's super important. There's nothing worse than letting a good conversation stretch out until it becomes something else. Something… um… less good.

But if you remember to always end conversations at the peak, you'll be just fine.

CONCLUSION

This book is a total and complete waste of your time.

I don't even know why you're still reading it.

No, I'm just kidding. Obviously I wouldn't have written this book if I didn't feel like it had something valuable to contribute to your life.

But now I'm going to ask you to do something a little bit... odd.

I want you to take everything that we've learned about today and flush it down the toilet. Totally erase it from your memory. Never think about it again.

I've given you a lot of different dating techniques today. But none of them can even compare to the Ultimate Dating Technique, as I like to call it.

Which is this: *there are no dating techniques.*

Just go out there and be yourself.

You're awesome. And the ladies will recognize that if you allow yourself to shine.

Don't get so caught up in trying to follow all of my advice that you forget the Ultimate Dating Technique.

If a girl can tell that you're following the advice from a dating book, then you've failed miserably. Just loosen up, have fun, and enjoy yourself. And make sure that the girl that you're with is enjoying herself as well.

And you'll be good.

I've said it before, and I'll say it again: dating isn't rocket science. Don't stress out too much. Remember what we've learned today, but don't obsess over it. Play it by ear. Use it when it suits you, and don't when it doesn't. I won't be offended.

And above all else, remember the Ultimate Dating Technique.

So yeah.

That's that.

I hope you've enjoyed this book.

I've sure had a heck of a fun time writing it, as I'm sure you can tell.

Finally, one more important point that I want to make before I officially leave you forever is this: don't be a slacker.

We've talked about a lot of awesome stuff today. The techniques that I've shown you are all that you need to totally nail the first interaction with any girl. Now go out there and make it happen. You're never ever gonna be glad that you stayed home and sat on your butt and watched Netflix. But if you suck it up and go out there and meet a nice girl and make something happen…well, yeah. You're gonna be glad you did.

So get off your lazy butt. I'm telling you, the only thing that separates the action-takers from the Netflix-watchers is the 2 seconds that it takes to stand up.

So do it.

Stand up, walk out the front door, and go have the time of your life.

Girls are awesome. And so are you. They deserve a guy like you. Now go out there and give 'em what they want.

25282041R00020

Printed in Great Britain
by Amazon